D0118766

Mammals

LONDON, NEW YORK, MUNICH,
MELBOURNE, and DELHI

Written and edited by Sarah Walker
and Anna Lofthouse
Designed by Jacqueline Gooden

Publishing manager Susan Leonard
Managing art editor Cathy Chesson
Senior editor Caroline Bingham
Jacket design Chris Drew
Picture researcher Brenda Clynch
Production Shivani Pandey
DTP Designer Almudena Díaz
Consultant Nick Lindsay

First American Edition, 2002
03 04 05 10 9 8 7 6 5 4 3 2

Published in the United States by
DK Publishing, Inc.
375 Hudson Street
New York, New York 10014

Library of Congress Cataloging-in-Publication Data

Walker, Sarah.
Mammals / by Sarah Walker—1st American ed.
p. cm. -- (Eye wonder)
Summary: Presents an overview of mammals, including their history, various kinds, physical characteristics, behavior, and endangered and extinct species.
ISBN 0-7894-8869-8 (plc) -- ISBN 0-7894-8900-7 (alb)
1. Mammals--Juvenile literature. [1. Mammals.] I. Title. II. Series.

QL706.2 .W35 2002
559--dc21

2002073390

Color reproduction by Colorscan, Singapore
Printed and bound in Italy by L.E.G.O.

See our complete
product line at
www.dk.com

Contents

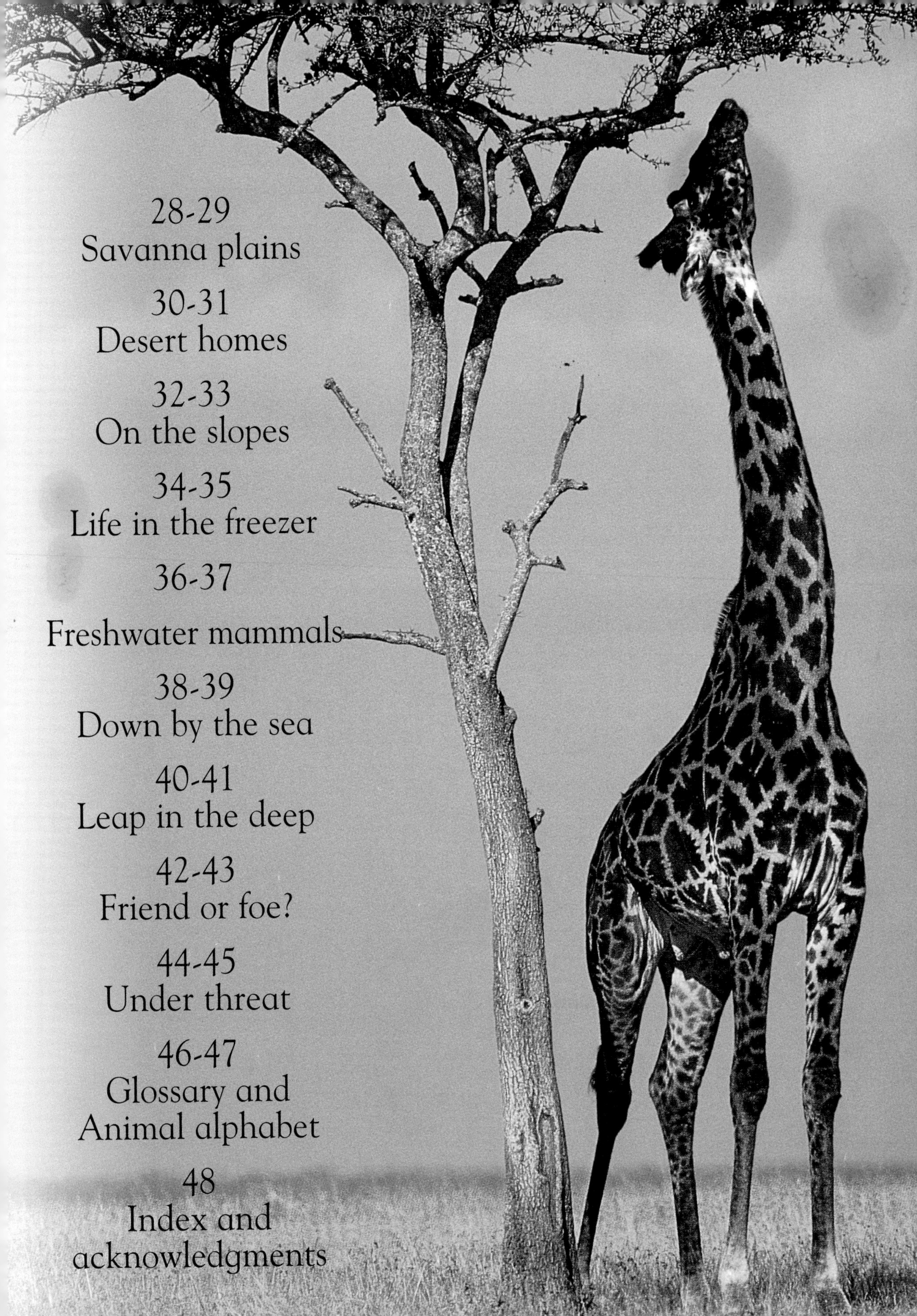

Mammal world

You might wonder if tiny mice, huge whales, and humans have anything in common. They do – they are all mammals. All mammals have hair or fur, are warm-blooded and have a constant body temperature, and feed their young on milk

Odd eggs out

Most mammals are born, but the hedgehoglike echidnas (see right) and the duck-billed platypus hatch from eggs.

Instant food

Almost all female mammals suckle their young on milk. The milk provides the best balance of fat and protein so that young mammals can grow quickly.

The human species is just one of the 4,000 or so

Hair (or fur) helps to keep heat in.

Long Haul...

Elephant moms are mammal record breakers for having the longest pregnancies – nearly two years! Young elephant calves grow inside their mothers like a lot of other mammals (for example, human babies, or kittens). When born, a calf can weigh 200 lbs (90 kg). So at the end of the pregnancy that's like a mom carrying 40 bags of sugar!

Kid mammals

Humans belong to a group of mammals called primates. Other primates include monkeys and apes, so they are our closest mammal relatives.

Open wide

Hippopotamuses would be perfect at the dentist's with a large mouth and a wide jaw stretch. All mammals have distinct jaws, meaning that the lower jaw is hinged directly to the skull.

ncredible mammal species on the planet Earth.

Mammals are the only animals to have ear flaps.

Amazing mammals

Mammals come in all shapes and sizes, but those that look alike belong to the same group, or order. Each order contains different types, or species, of mammal.

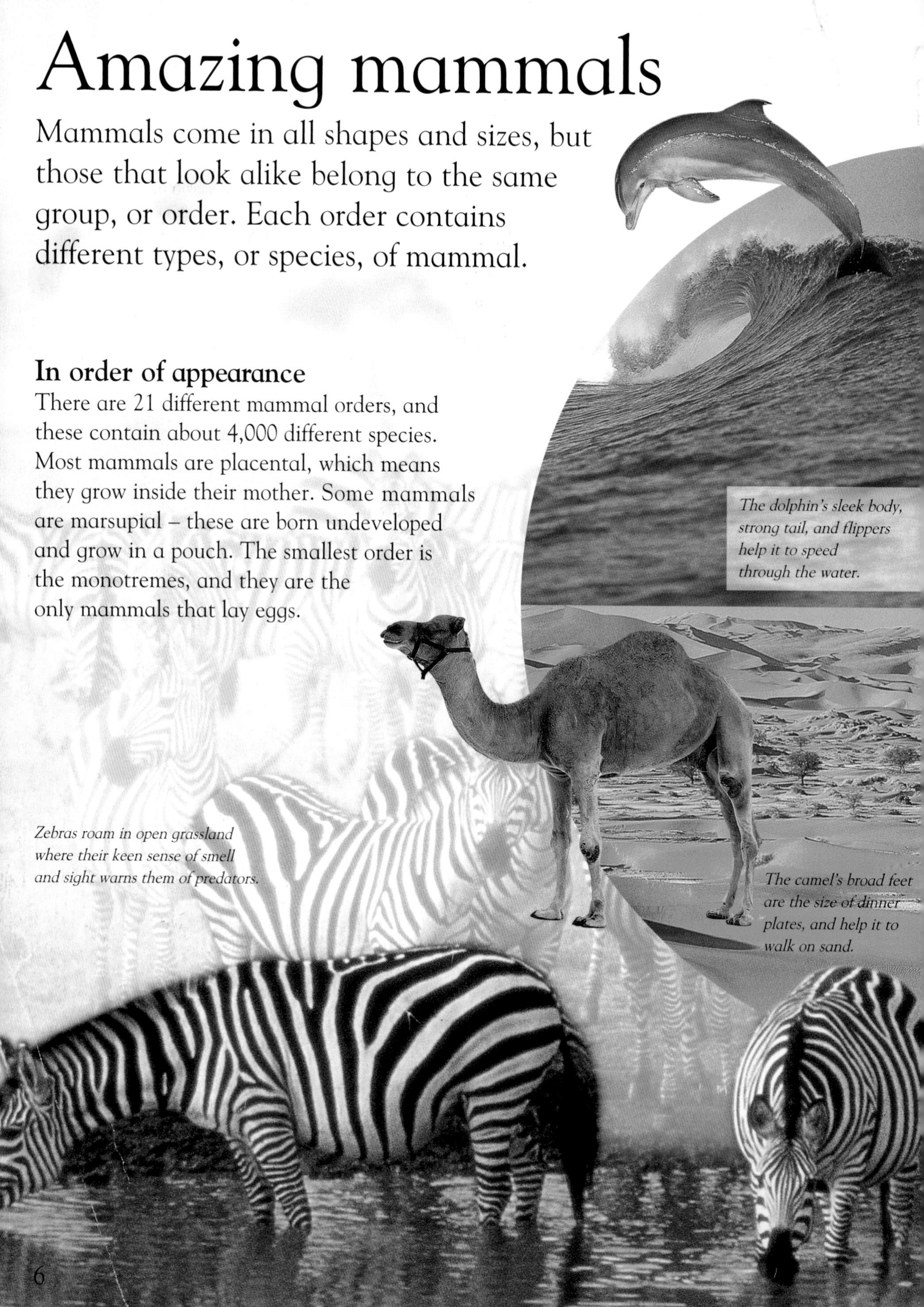

In order of appearance

There are 21 different mammal orders, and these contain about 4,000 different species. Most mammals are placental, which means they grow inside their mother. Some mammals are marsupial – these are born undeveloped and grow in a pouch. The smallest order is the monotremes, and they are the only mammals that lay eggs.

The dolphin's sleek body, strong tail, and flippers help it to speed through the water.

Zebras roam in open grassland where their keen sense of smell and sight warns them of predators.

The camel's broad feet are the size of dinner plates, and help it to walk on sand.

Where do mammals live?

Mammals can be found almost everywhere, from the frozen wastes of the Arctic to the dry heat of a barren desert. Most live on land, but some live in water. All are well adapted to the surroundings, or habitat, in which they live.

Amazing mammals

- Bone fossils show that mammals first lived on Earth about 200 million years ago.
- The reason mammals are *not* floppy like jelly is because they are vertebrates (animals with backbones).
- Rodents are the largest order, with 1,702 species.

The polar bear's thick fleecy coat protects it from the icy Arctic winds.

The jaguar's coat helps it to blend into the background in the lush rain forests.

Mammal Medalists

In a mammal Olympics the medals would go to the following: the *sloth* for being the *slowest* competitor – moving at less than 1 mph (2 kph); the *skunk* for making the *stinkiest* smell; the *pygmy shrew* for weighing in as the *smallest* at just 1/16-1/8 oz (2-3 g).

Family life

Some mammals choose to stay in family groups, making it easier for them to find food and defend themselves. Mammal parents spend longer with their young than other animals.

Playtime tussles
Female lions live in permanent groups called prides and look after each other's cubs. The cubs play-fight, which is how they learn to hunt.

Meerkat watch

A gang of meerkats varies from five to 30 members. They are very protective of their home, or territory, and have different roles, such as sentry duty or babysitting.

African elephants are the biggest land mammals.

Amazing mammals

- There are about 60,000 muscles in an elephant's trunk.
- A lion can devour 50 lb (23 kg) of meat in one meal. That's about 350 hotdogs.
- Ferocious fights can happen between rival meerkat gangs.

An elephant's tusks are just overgrown teeth.

Female families

Female elephants and their children stay close together in family herds. The biggest female, the matriarch, leads them wherever they go.

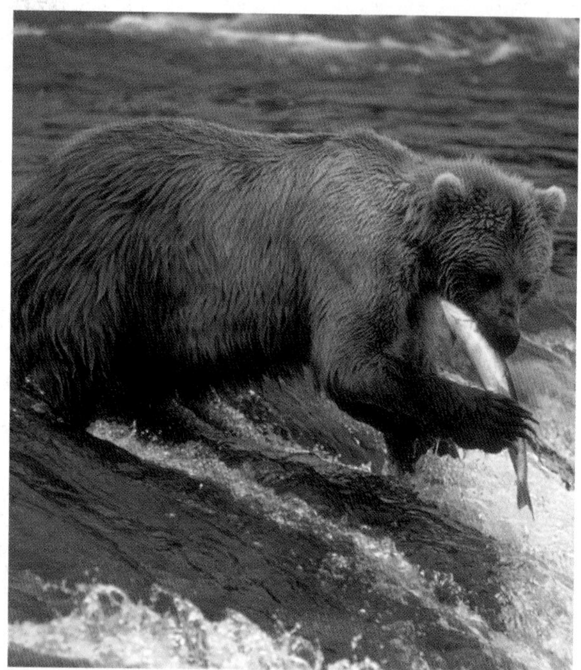

Different diets

What do you prefer? Vegetables, meat, fish, or a little of everything? Mammals eat all kinds of things. They eat because they need energy, just like a car needs fuel to go.

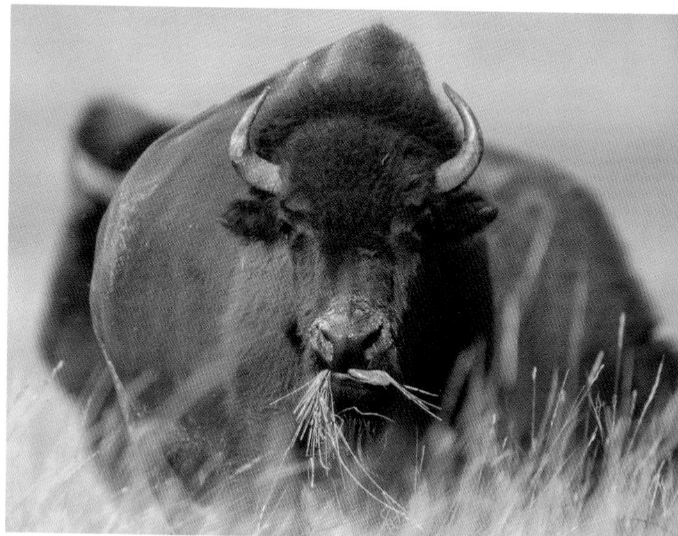

A mixed plate

This Alaskan brown bear, like other brown bears, eats a meat and plant, or omnivorous, diet. It waits to pounce on any salmon swimming upstream, but also chomps on plants, fungi, and large insects.

Keep on chewing

American bison are herbivores, which means they only eat plants. They graze on grass. Then they rest. Then they chew on the grass even more.

Wild mammals build their daily routine around finding enough to eat.

Make mine meat

A pack of gray wolves maul their hunting prize. As one of the world's best-known carnivores, or meat eaters, their bodies are designed for hunting other animals. They have powerful jaws and sharp teeth.

Don't stick your tongue out!

Giant anteaters wouldn't listen to this warning. They use their 2 ft (60 cm) spiked and sticky tongues to ensnare termites and ants once their clawed front feet have ripped open the nests.

The anteater pushes its long, tubelike snout into the hole.

Amazing mammals

- Wolves can eat up to 20 lb (9 kg) of meat in one meal.
- A giant anteater flicks out its tongue 150 times a minute.
- Brown bears eat a lot. The extra weight helps them survive the winter, when they sleep, or hibernate, for several months.

Moonlighters

Just as you are going to sleep some creatures are waking up, more than ready for the night. Nocturnal mammals often have special features – such as big eyes for seeing well in the dark.

Night babies

Bush babies have large eyes for night vision and batlike ears that help them to track insect prey in the dark.

The ringtailed cat is an excellent climber and hunts in trees for small birds.

Is it really a cat?

No! The ringtailed cat is part of the raccoon family. Like the red fox, it hunts alone at night.

TALE OF ALL TAILS!

Around the world, people like telling stories about me because they can't decide if I'm cunning or intelligent. In Ancient Greece, Aesop wrote about me in fables. In the US, I am Brer Fox who tries to outwit Brer Rabbit; and in Japan I am revered as a messenger of the Shinto rice goddess.

Night raiders

Red foxes usually hunt alone at night in woodland or open country, and increasingly in built-up areas. They will eat almost anything.

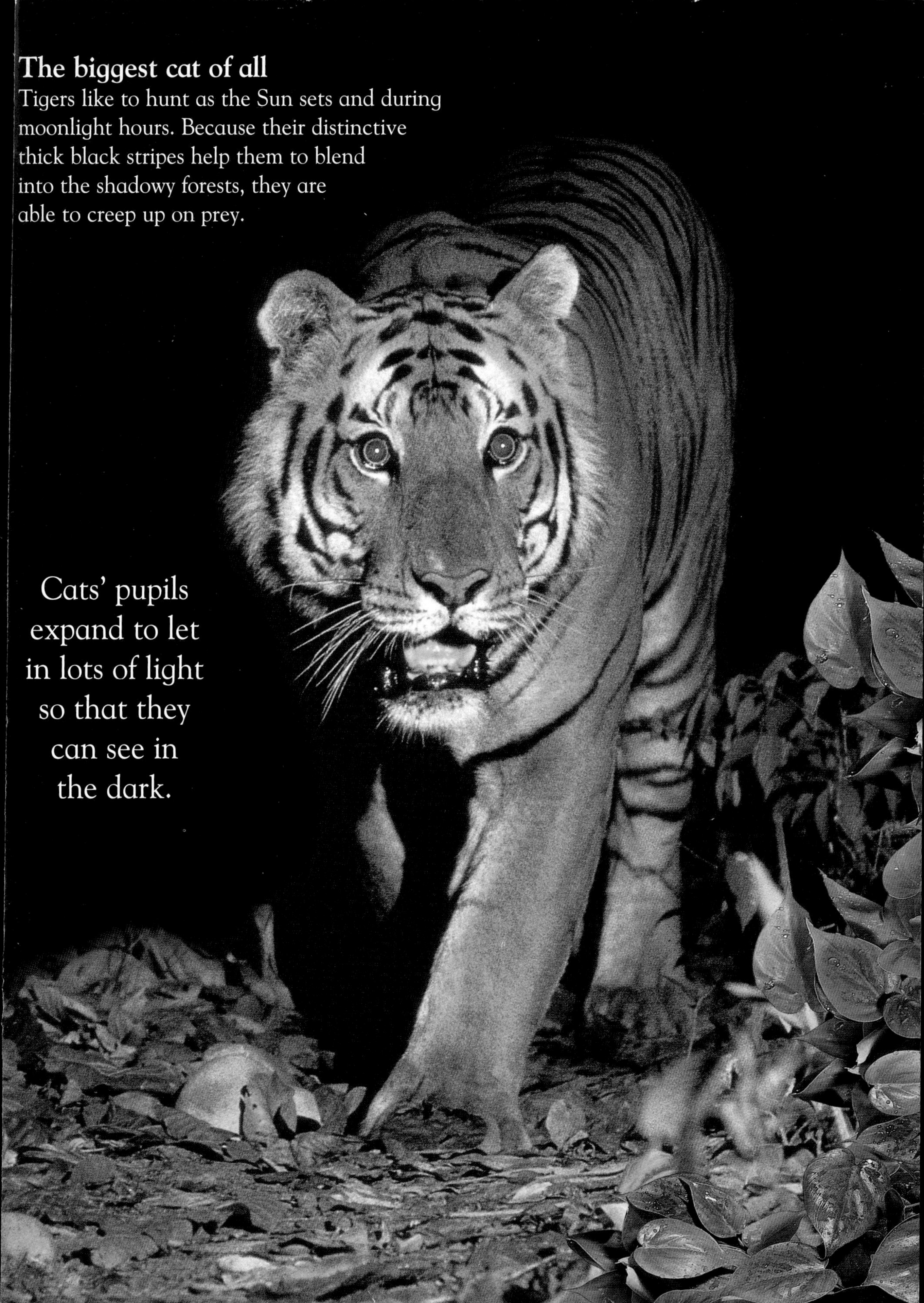

The biggest cat of all

Tigers like to hunt as the Sun sets and during moonlight hours. Because their distinctive thick black stripes help them to blend into the shadowy forests, they are able to creep up on prey.

Cats' pupils expand to let in lots of light so that they can see in the dark.

On the defensive

When under attack all mammals have ways of defending themselves. After all, none of them want to be eaten or hurt. Some will turn and run, while others will use unusual methods to put off a predator.

Is it or isn't it?

Virginia opossums often play dead when under threat, hoping that the potential predator does not want to eat a dead animal! They may lie still for up to six hours.

A living ball

If threatened, the Brazilian three-banded armadillo rolls itself up into a complete ball, protecting its soft parts. Tough skin and an awkward shape prove an effective defense against most predators.

No way through

These enormous musk oxen form a defensive line or circle if threatened by a polar bear or wolf pack. Young or weak animals are protected in the middle of the group.

Fully grown adults may leave the line to charge an attacker.

Amazing mammals

- Brazilian three-banded armadillos can curl up as soon as they are born.
- When an opossum "plays dead," its heartbeat slows down.
- If gorillas are threatened, they may attempt to avoid the danger by quickly heading into thick forest. This is called "silent flight."

Gentle giant?

The lowland gorilla is not an aggressive mammal, and what looks like a scary roar is actually a nervous yawn! Male gorillas will protect their social group. Defense tactics include roaring and beating their chests.

Underground, overground

Many mammals have underground homes or burrows where they have their babies and hide in when there's danger. Most leave their burrows to find food or water, but some, like the mole, are true burrowers and rarely leave the earth.

Underground towns

Colonies, or towns, of black-tailed prairie dogs live in tunnels under grassland that may be an incredible 16 ft (5 m) deep. Prairie dogs line their nesting chambers with soft grass and dig out passing places along the tunnels.

Busy burrow

Rabbits are sociable creatures and love to live in large colonies. Their burrows are large and complicated. They even have emergency exits!

Born to dig
You'll know there's a mole around if you see mole hills – a series of soft hills that the mole pushes up. Their huge front feet make them perfect little diggers.

Tunnel vision
A pocket gopher spends most of its life underground. Its small eyes and ears, flat head, and long whiskers are all useful in a burrow.

Midnight feast!
These tiny wood mice are nibbling on acorns in the safety of their burrow. Their varied diet also includes berries, worms, fruits, and snails.

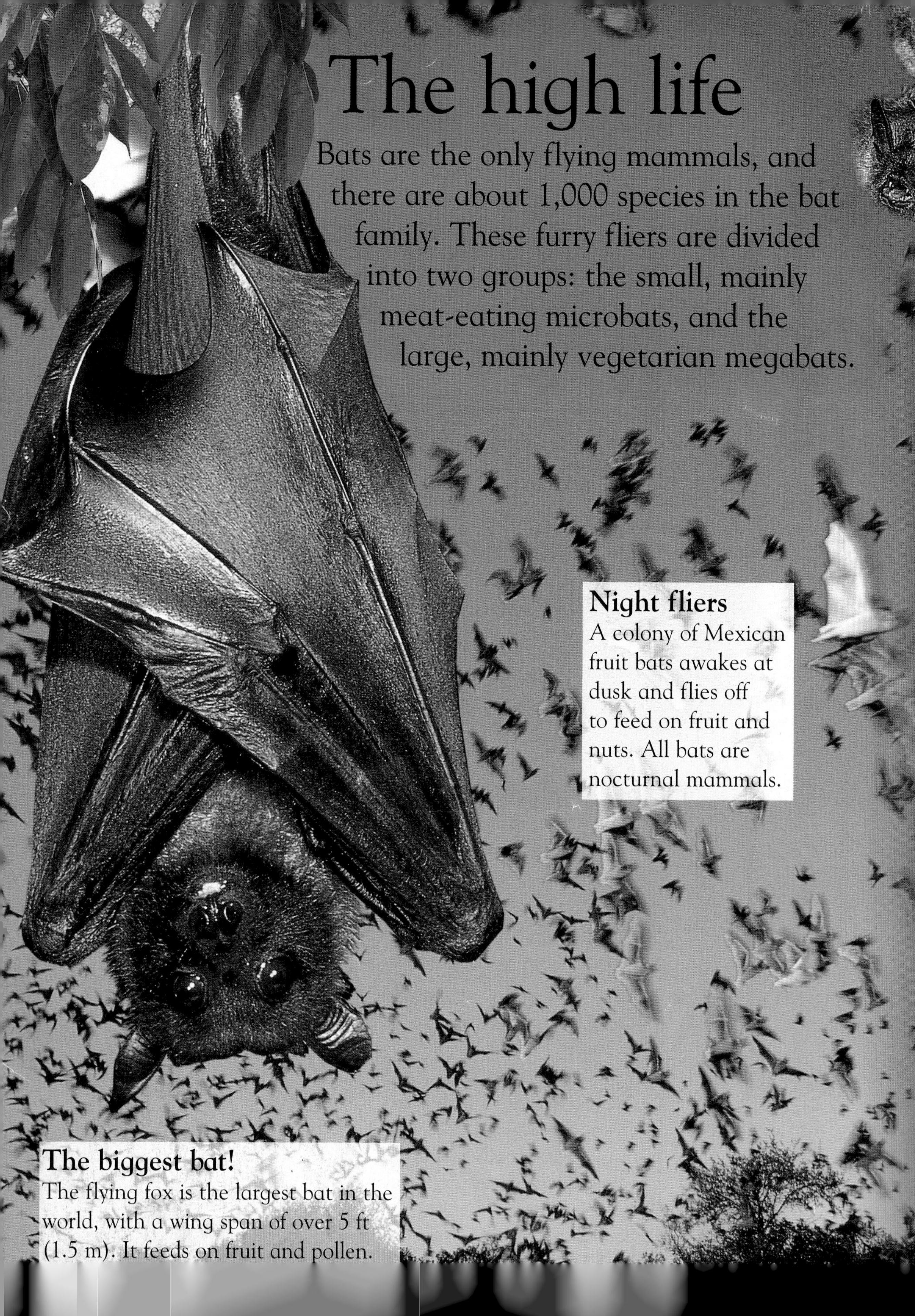

The high life

Bats are the only flying mammals, and there are about 1,000 species in the bat family. These furry fliers are divided into two groups: the small, mainly meat-eating microbats, and the large, mainly vegetarian megabats.

Night fliers
A colony of Mexican fruit bats awakes at dusk and flies off to feed on fruit and nuts. All bats are nocturnal mammals.

The biggest bat!
The flying fox is the largest bat in the world, with a wing span of over 5 ft (1.5 m). It feeds on fruit and pollen.

Roosting together

Bats often gather together in huge numbers at a single site. This may be a cave, an old building, or a hollow tree. The site must provide the bats with shelter and protection from predators.

Bloodsucker

This vampire bat is enjoying a tasty snack of donkey blood. Its sharp teeth easily pierce the skin, and its spit prevents the blood from clotting. Only three species of bat feed on blood.

FINDING FOOD

Most insect-eating bats hunt using a process called echolocation. Each bat makes a series of clicks, and this sound is carried out into the air. This noise bounces off any potential prey, such as mosquitoes and moths, and sends information back to the bat. The bat can then find the prey, and enjoy its meal!

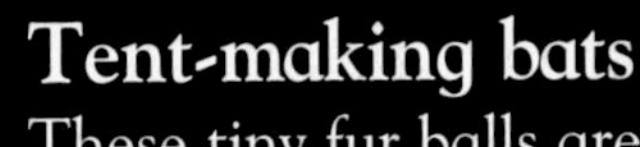

Tent-making bats

These tiny fur balls are Honduran white bats. They only appear white under artificial light and are well camouflaged in the murky rain forest. They create shelters from large rain-forest leaves.

Primate party

Apes, monkeys, and humans are the most well-known members of a mammal group called primates. A primate party would be a swinging one since primates are playful and highly intelligent creatures.

A devoted mother

An orangutan mother and baby stay together for about eight years. The baby clings to its mother's fur as she moves through the trees. At night the mother makes nests from leaves for her baby and her to sleep in.

Gentle giants

Gorillas live in family groups. They weigh in as the heaviest of all the primates, but despite appearances are peaceful vegetarians. Their enthusiasm for eating forest plants can result in large pot bellies.

A gripping tail

Many Central and South American monkeys – such as this black howler monkey – use their grasping, or prehensile, tail as a fifth limb. With its very distinctive howl, it is one of the loudest primates.

Second in the class

Humans score highest for intelligence, but chimpanzees are second. This chimp is using a stone as a tool for cracking open palm nuts.

If you scratch my back...

...I'll scratch yours. These baboons are checking each other's fur for ticks and lice. It is part of a behavior shared by most primates called grooming. This also helps the primates to develop good friendships.

Amazing mammals

- The orangutan's name comes from the Malay words for "man of the wood."
- Do you like making faces? Many primates can make faces to show their feelings and to communicate with each other.

Amazing marsupials

Kangaroos and koalas belong to a group of mammals called marsupials. A marsupial is only partly formed when it is born, and it continues to grow in a pocket, called a pouch, on the outside of its mother's stomach.

Mobile homes

A baby kangaroo or joey is born after just 12 days inside its mother. It crawls through its mother's fur and into a special place called a pouch. It stays in its mother's pouch, drinking her milk, for the next six months.

When the kangaroo hops, a long tail helps it to balance.

Thirsty work

A newborn kangaroo is blind, helpless, and very pink. It clings tightly to its mother's fur and will suckle continually.

Piggyback, please

A koala spends most of its life in eucalyptus trees. It sleeps for up to 18 hours a day and feeds only on eucalyptus leaves. A baby koala lives in its mother's pouch for about six months before crawling onto her back.

A fully grown kangaroo is as tall as an adult human, but at birth, it is less than ¾ inch (2 cm) long.

Powerful kangaroos

The largest living marsupials, red kangaroos live in Australia. They live in groups of about two to 10 animals, with one dominant male and several females. When bounding at full speed, kangaroos can reach speeds of about 30 mph (50 kph).

WINNER TAKES THE GIRL

Male kangaroos sometimes fight over females. This fighting can take the form of "boxing." The kangaroos stand up on their hind legs and attempt to push their opponent off balance by jabbing him or locking forearms. The winner of the boxing match is the stronger male, and he gets the girl!

Deep in the jungle

Imagine a place where it rains every day but where it is uncomfortably hot and sticky. Many mammals make a good home here – among the towering trees of the rain forest.

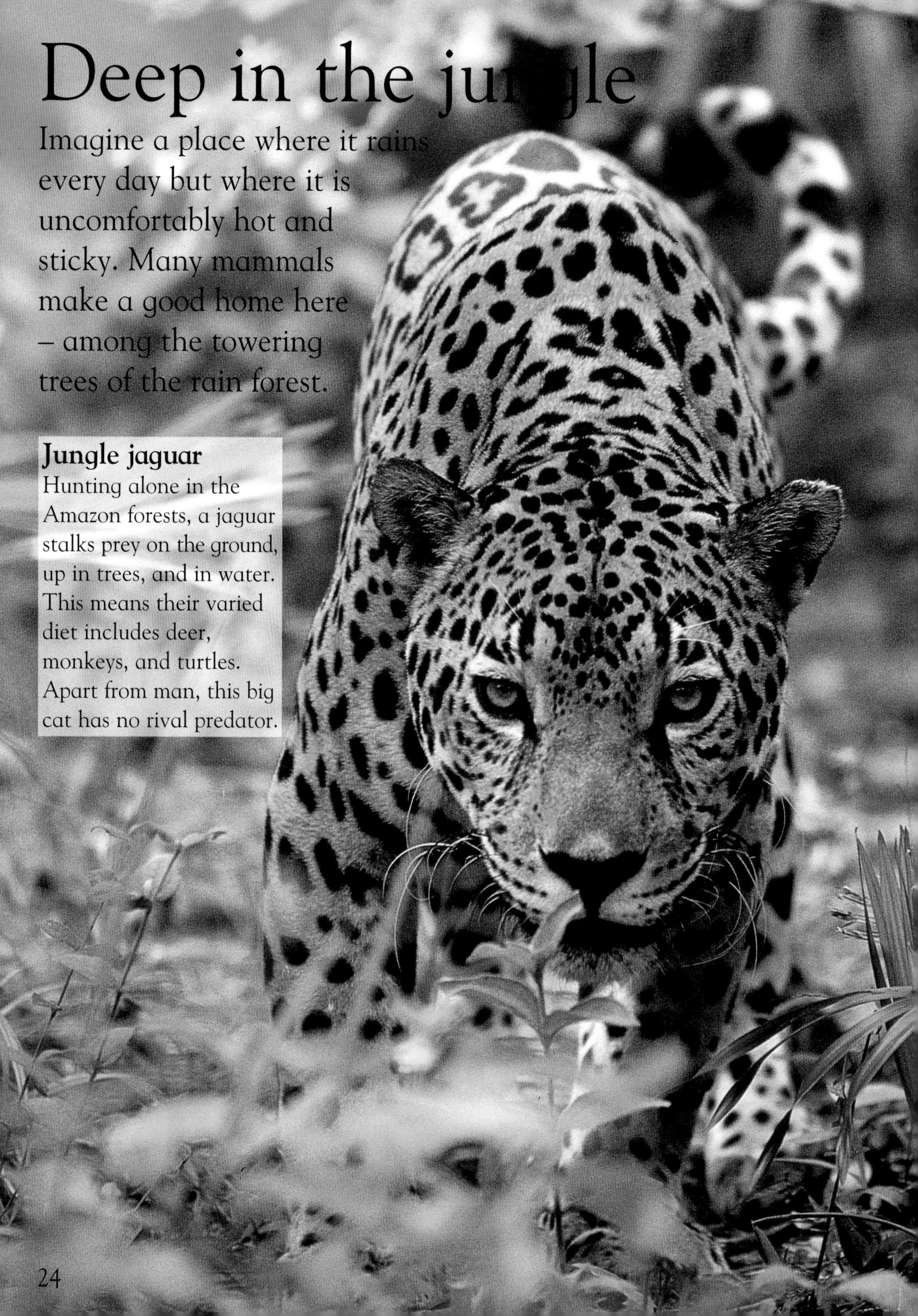

Jungle jaguar
Hunting alone in the Amazon forests, a jaguar stalks prey on the ground, up in trees, and in water. This means their varied diet includes deer, monkeys, and turtles. Apart from man, this big cat has no rival predator.

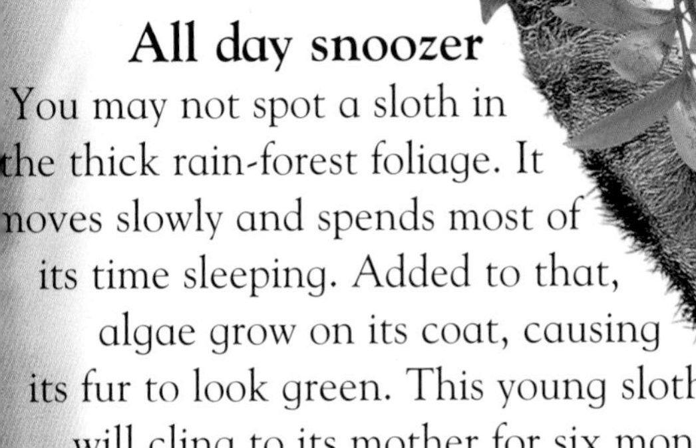

All day snoozer

You may not spot a sloth in the thick rain-forest foliage. It moves slowly and spends most of its time sleeping. Added to that, algae grow on its coat, causing its fur to look green. This young sloth will cling to its mother for six months.

Hooked up

A silky anteater's hooklike claws are ideal for gripping a branch. It uses its red, sticky, saliva-coated tongue to scoop up ants from their nests.

Amazing mammals

- The sloth is one of the sleepiest mammals in the world. It will doze in a tree for between 15 – 18 hours a day.
- A silky anteater can eat up to 8,000 ants in one day.
- Jaguars go for a direct kill, biting through the skull of their opponent rather than seizing its neck.

Trunklike noses give tapirs a good sense of smell.

In the swim

Find a rain forest river or swamp and you may spot a tapir. These timid creatures like to cool off in water, and use it to hide from predators.

Eye eye!

Pads on the ends of a tarsier's fingers and toes help it to grip a branch while its big eyes scan the forest floor for insects to eat. Can you believe that each eye is heavier than its brain!

Forest-dwellers

Unlike a rain forest, a temperate forest is ruled by the seasons – as are its mammals. In the warm spring, the young are born. In the summer they feed and grow. Chilly fall days see thicker coats. To survive the cold winter, some sleep or hibernate.

What's for dinner?

One of the largest wild pigs, the wild boar spends many happy hours rooting around on the forest floor. It is looking for anything to eat, from roots and nuts to small animals.

Snack stop

Each fall, red squirrels scurry around gathering nuts and pinecones. They'll store these provisions in the ground or in tree holes, raiding these "cupboards" in the winter when food is scarce.

Sleep tight

The dormouse doesn't even try to struggle through winter. It curls up, snuggles down into its leaf and grass nest, and sleeps, or hibernates, the winter away.

In fall, the antlers fall off and regrow in the spring. They grow bigger each year.

Amazing mammals

- Dormice are named after the Latin word for sleep: *dormire*. They spend an amazing three-quarters of their year "asleep"!
- A moose has broad hooves that enable it to move through snow, muddy bogs, and lakes.
- The wild boar is the ancestor of the domestic pig.

Moosing around

The elk, or moose, is the largest member of the deer family. The male is huge. Its antlers alone can span up to $6\frac{1}{2}$ ft (2 m). Forests with swampy areas provide the moose with all its food, but just imagine eating twigs or the roots of water plants!

Savanna plains

Africa's tropical grassland, or savanna, is home to spectacular groups of mammals. Life is hot and there is little rainfall, but grasses keep on growing for much of the year and grow back quickly after being nibbled on by the grazing herds.

Tongue stretch

Giraffes are the tallest animals in the world. Some males grow up to 18 ft (5.5 m) tall. Their long necks allow them to reach tasty leaves high up in the trees.

Predatory pride

Lions hunt many grassland mammals, even attacking young elephants and giraffes. They live in prides of five to 40 animals. Prides are made up mostly of adult females and their cubs, and include a few males.

All species of giraffe have different markings.

Amazing mammals

- Each zebra has a unique stripe pattern.
- Lionesses provide each other with a babysitting service for their cubs!
- Giraffes can gallop at speeds of 30 mph (50kph).

Giraffe splits!

The short, wet season produces water holes that shrink as the year progresses. This drives groups such as giraffes to travel great distances to find them. Their height means that they have to stretch their front legs very wide in order to drink.

Safety in numbers

Zebras often mingle with wildebeest for mutual defense. No one knows why they have stripes, but it could be to confuse predators or for their own temperature control.

Desert homes

The Sun burns down. There is no water, and very little food. At last the Sun sets, but it is now bitterly cold. Welcome to the desert. Surprisingly, a number of mammals love it here!

Where's the water?

The spinifex hopping mouse doesn't need to drink. It gets all the moisture it needs by nibbling on plant food.

Ships of the desert

Camels are ideal desert mammals whether they have one hump or two. They can survive for weeks and travel long distances without food or water, an ability that makes them useful for carrying things. That's why they are known as the ships of the desert.

Camels have padded feet for protection against the hot ground.

Cool grazers

During the heat of the day, Arabian oryx can be spotted huddled under trees. Their bright white coats reflect the light back, and therefore help to keep them cool. There were hardly any oryx left in the 1970s, but captive breeding has meant that hundreds have been returned to the wild.

Deserts cover about 20% of the Earth's land.

A double row of eyelashes keep the sand out of a camel's eyes.

Thirsty work

Contrary to popular belief, a camel's hump is not full of water. It is actually made of fat, which the camel can live from if there is no food or water. A camel can survive for 10 months without water and then drink a *lot* very quickly – similar to 340 cans of soda in 10 minutes!

On the slopes

A mountain slope is a tricky place to live. The weather gets colder as you head up and the air gets thinner, with less oxygen. And there's not a lot of food! But some mammals choose to make it their home.

A rocky home

Alpine marmots live high up in alpine meadows. If threatened, they make a loud piercing whistle. To survive the winter, they retreat to their burrows to sleep, or hibernate, for several months.

A sky-high leap

The mountain goat is an expert rock climber, and baby goats (kids) can walk and climb shortly after they are born. Their oval hooves have a rubberlike sole that helps them grip onto the slippery slopes.

Amazing mammals

- Japanese macaques are also known as "snow monkeys."
- The Alpine marmot is one of 14 species of marmot.
- The mountain goat looks like it has a beard like other goats, but it is actually just an extension of its throat mane.

Many mountain mammals have thick fur to protect them from the icy weather.

Jump in!

These striking Japanese macaques live in the cold highlands and mountains of Japan. In winter, temperatures drop below freezing. To stay warm, the clever monkeys have learned to take a bath in the natural hot springs.

Life in the freezer

The polar regions, at the top and bottom of the world, are tough places for mammals. They need to survive the freezing temperatures, especially in winter. They also need to be cunning to find what little food there is.

Boxing bunnies

Arctic hares have white winter coats to help hide them from predators. They have no trouble finding each other, though! The males box to claim a female.

Young polar bears spend up to two years with their mothers.

Polar giants

The enormous polar bear is one of the world's largest land-based carnivores. It has thick, white fur, which keeps it warm in the freezing cold and camouflages it in the white snow. Polar bears give birth to cubs in the winter in secure ice dens.

Made for snow

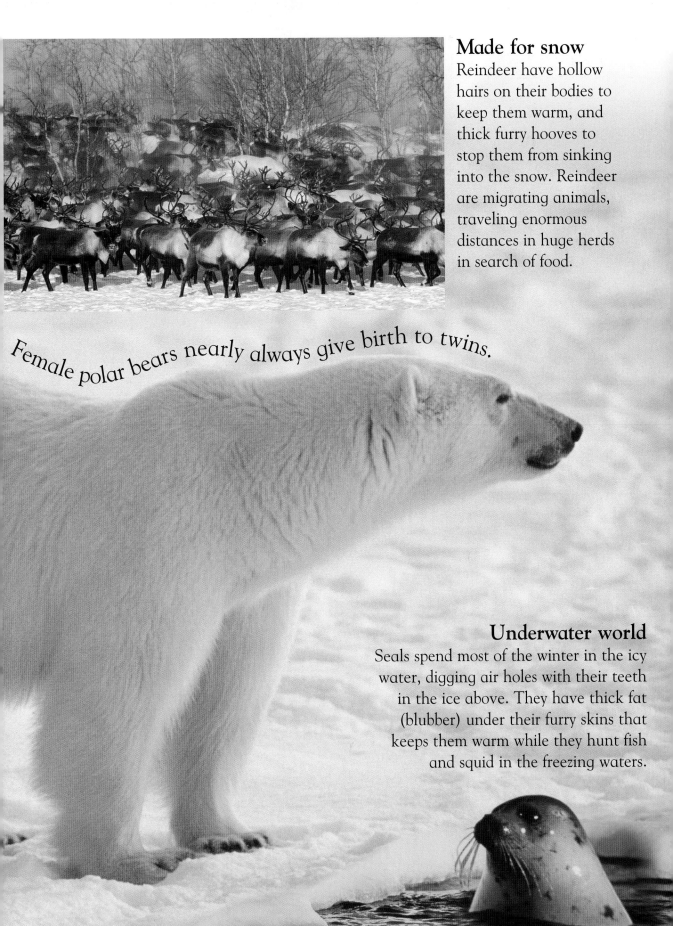

Reindeer have hollow hairs on their bodies to keep them warm, and thick furry hooves to stop them from sinking into the snow. Reindeer are migrating animals, traveling enormous distances in huge herds in search of food.

Female polar bears nearly always give birth to twins.

Underwater world

Seals spend most of the winter in the icy water, digging air holes with their teeth in the ice above. They have thick fat (blubber) under their furry skins that keeps them warm while they hunt fish and squid in the freezing waters.

Freshwater mammals

Fast-flowing freshwater rivers and streams, large lakes, and boggy marshes are home to all kinds of mammals. But although well adapted to water, they all have to come to the surface to breathe.

An underwater playground

Otters are well suited to water, with webbed paws, streamlined bodies, and ears and noses that close when the otter dives. These playful mammals often chase each other, and dive for rocks and shells.

The river dolphin

This friendly-looking mammal lives in the Amazon River in South America. It swims through the slow-moving river channels, looking for fish and crabs. Sometimes it swims upside down so it can see what's happening underneath.

Amazing mammals

- Otters and beavers belong to the Mustelidae family, which also includes minks, stoats, skunks, and badgers.
- The name hippopotamus means "river horse."
- An Amazon River dolphin has 25–30 pairs of teeth.

Beavers are often thought of as pests, as they dam rivers and streams.

Lazing around. . .

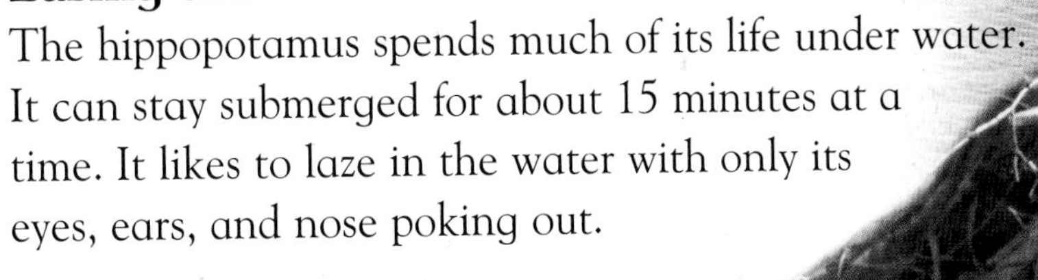

The hippopotamus spends much of its life under water. It can stay submerged for about 15 minutes at a time. It likes to laze in the water with only its eyes, ears, and nose poking out.

The busy beaver

Beavers are nature's builders. They construct homes out of mud and branches, complete with underwater entrances. A series of dams built around the home controls the flow of water, so beavers have their own private pool.

Beavers drag the branches into place with their strong jaws.

Down by the sea

The shallow waters around the world's oceans provide a home for many mammals. Some divide their time between swimming in the sea, and breeding and caring for young on the shores. Others never leave the ocean.

Amazing mammals

- Seals, sea lions, and walruses belong to the "pinniped" family.
- The only pinnipeds able to support themselves in a semi-upright position on land are sea lions, fur seals, and walruses.
- Walruses turn pink when they leave the cold sea and their bodies warm up in the sun.

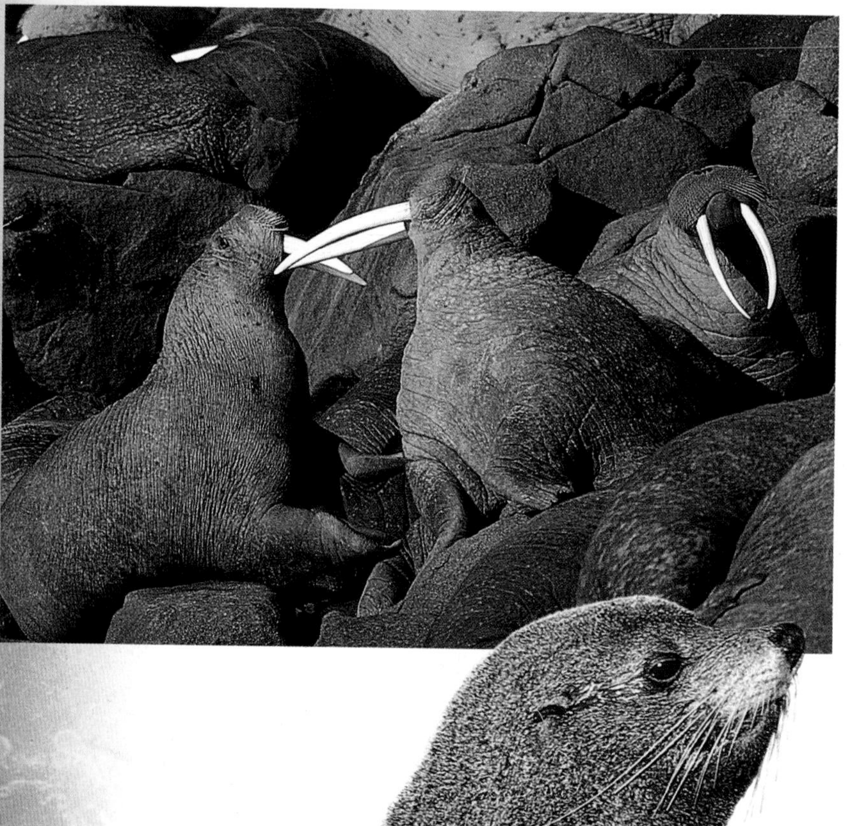

Battle of the tusks

These large, male walruses are using their long, sharp tusks to fight over a female. Older males are often covered in scars from previous, bloody battles.

The tusks of male walruses can grow to about 3 ft (1 m) in length.

Nearly all pinnipeds are covered in a layer of fat known as blubber.

A furry tale

Although seals appear sleek and shiny when they are under the water, they actually have two layers of soft fur. Adult fur is not as thick as baby fur, and some seal species are furrier than others. Fur keeps seals warm and is waterproof.

Dugongs were alive in the time of the dinosaurs.

A streamlined body makes all pinnipeds agile swimmers.

Underwater grazer

The dugong is also known as a "sea cow" because it grazes on the seabed for sea-grass roots. These large, vegetarian mammals spend all of their lives in the sea, only coming to the surface to breathe.

Swimming sea lions

California sea lions are fast swimmers and can move at 25 mph (40 kph) in short bursts. They can stay under water for up to an hour using air that is stored in their lungs.

Leap in the deep

The ocean-dwelling cetaceans are some of the most specialized mammals in the world. The cetacean family includes all whales, dolphins, and porpoises. All have streamlined bodies, can dive deeply, and can hold their breath underwater for long periods of time.

Leaping high

Bottlenose dolphins are found in all of the world's oceans, except the polar regions. Living in groups, or schools, of between four and 20 animals, these playful mammals often leap above the waves.

Amazing mammals

- There are two types of whales. Baleen whales, which filter food through plates in their mouths, and toothed whales, such as killer whales.
- All cetaceans breathe through nostrils on their heads.
- Water supports a whale's weight; if whales lived on land they would be too big to survive.
- A humpback whale calf can grow until it is approximately 50 ft (16 m) long.

Breaching giants

This humpback whale is leaping high out of the water. This leaping is known as breaching. All whales breach, and we don't really know why they do this. It may be to warn off other whales, to communicate with their group, or just for fun. A whale this enormous will make a huge splash when it hits the water.

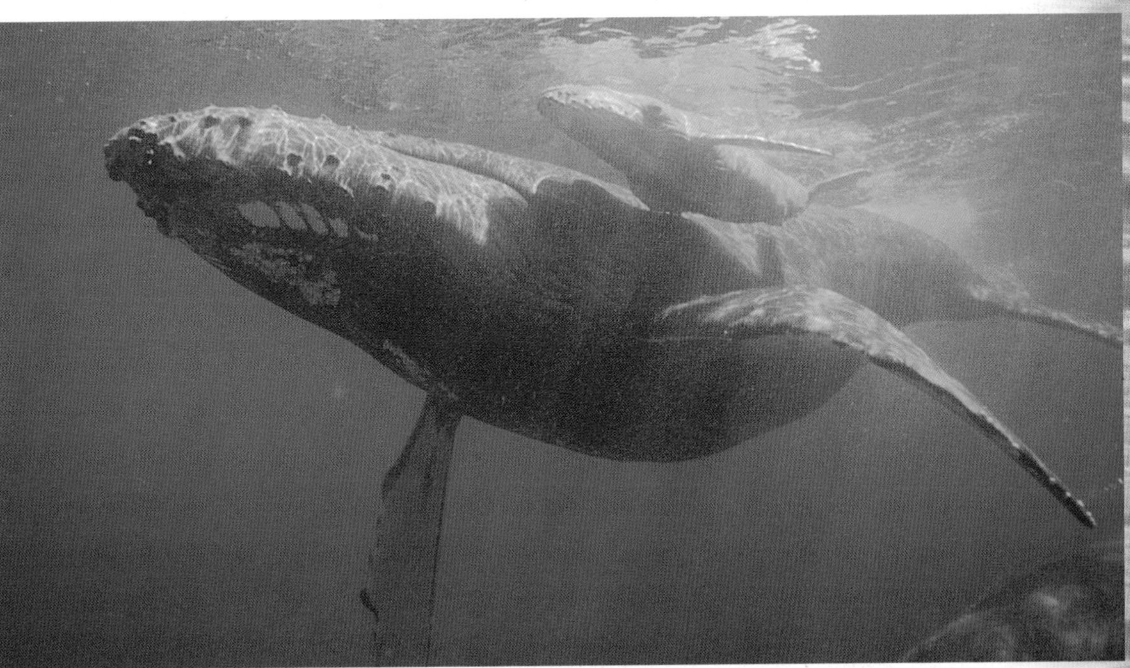

Water baby

Humpback whales tend to have their calves in the spring, in warm, tropical waters. The calf is born tail first, and its mother helps it to the surface so it can breathe. The calf will stay with its mother for about a year.

Friend or foe?

As in any big family, sometimes everyone gets along, and sometimes they don't! Humans can have close or useful relationships with other mammals. But there are also times when mammals can cause problems.

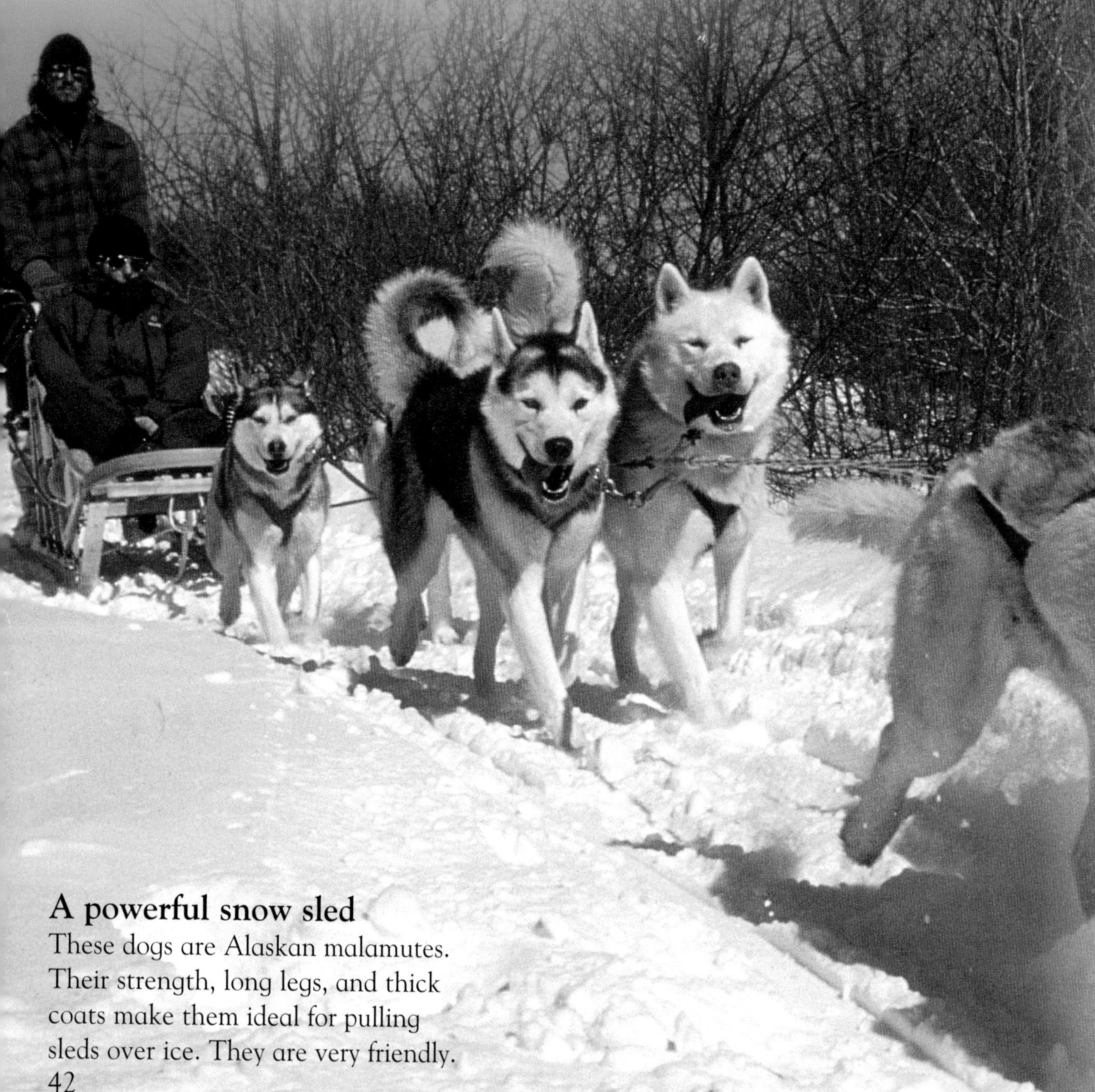

A powerful snow sled

These dogs are Alaskan malamutes. Their strength, long legs, and thick coats make them ideal for pulling sleds over ice. They are very friendly.

Pesty nibblers

Some people keep mice as pets, but others squeal and are scared at the very sight of them. House mice can wreak havoc; they spoil food if they get a chance to nibble, and they can eat through books and wires and spread disease.

Amazing mammals

- In New Zealand, sheep outnumber people by 20 to 1.
- To survive, mice breed very quickly. A house mouse can have 70 baby mice in a year.
- Pet kittens can look after themselves at about eight weeks, whereas cubs from big cats rely on Mom for longer!

Popular pets

Years ago, wild cats killed mice and rats that ate people's grain. Humans began to care for the friendly cats and soon they were pets.

A sheep haircut

Sheep were first used, or domesticated, by people many years ago for their wool, meat, and milk. Sheep are shorn once a year when their coats are at their thickest.

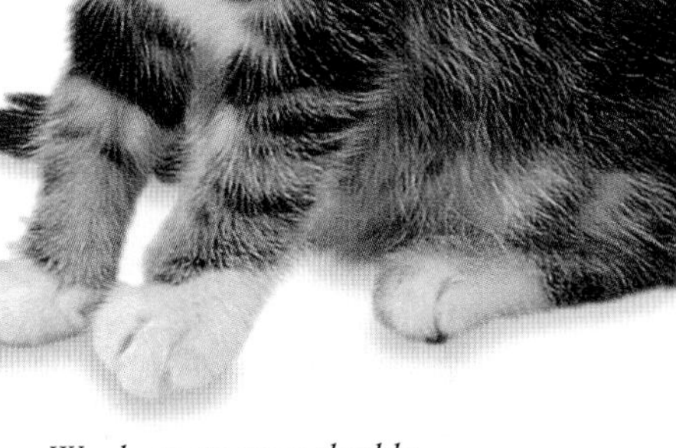

Wooly coats are valuable after they're spun into cloth or yarn for sweaters.

Under threat

Can you imagine having your home taken away or being hunted? Many mammals live with these threats all the time.

A watchful eye

Just as famous people have bodyguards, rhinoceroses have guards to protect them from poachers.

This black rhinoceros's horn can grow up to $4^1/2$ ft (1.4 m).

Shocking news

Rhinos are under threat because people kill them for their horns. The horns are used for making traditional Asian medicines and dagger handles.

A park for everyone

Large herds of bison wander and graze in safety in Yellowstone National Park in Wyoming. Nobody is allowed to shoot them. They share the park with many other mammals, including grizzly bears.

Amazing mammals

- 100 years ago, there were a million black rhinos. Now, only 2,400 are left.
- The Chimfunshi orphanage in Zambia looks after 80 chimpanzees.
- Pandas have an extra thumb for gripping bamboo stems.

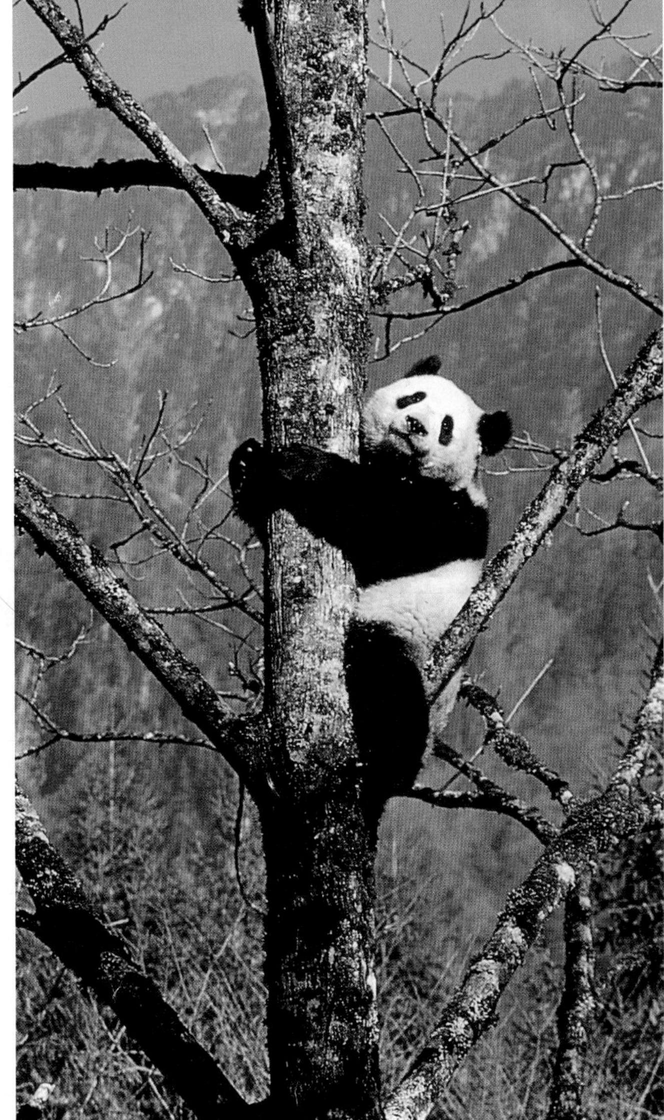

Pressures for pandas

A giant panda needs to munch on a variety of bamboo stems every day. However, habitat changes mean that there aren't enough types of bamboo plants. Reserves in China are trying to help.

Orphaned chimps quickly learn to feed from a bottle.

Feeding time

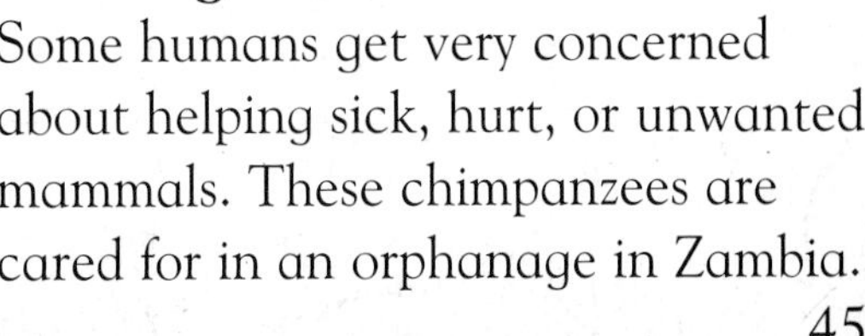

Some humans get very concerned about helping sick, hurt, or unwanted mammals. These chimpanzees are cared for in an orphanage in Zambia.

Glossary

Here are the meanings of some words it is useful to know when learning about mammals.

Camouflage a color or pattern that matches an animal's surroundings and helps disguise it.

Carnivore a meat eater.

Colony a group of animals that live together.

Echolocation a means of using echoes to steer an animal toward food and to build a picture of what is around them.

Habitat the place where a creature or plant naturally lives or grows.

Herbivore a plant eater.

Hibernate describes the period some animals spend asleep in the winter.

Marsupial mammals whose young are born undeveloped. They continue their development in a pouch.

Migration a long journey which some animals undergo each year to find better living conditions.

Nocturnal active at night.

Omnivore a plant and meat eater.

Predator an animal that hunts other animals for food.

Prey an animal hunted for food.

Prehensile tail a tail that can grasp (like a hand).

Stalk to approach prey quietly, so that they do not notice.

Suckle the means by which a baby mammal feeds from its mother.

Warm-blooded able to maintain a constant, warm body temperature, despite the surrounding temperature.

Animal alphabet

Each mammal featured in this book is listed here, along with its page number and which area it comes from.

Index

Acknowledgments

Dorling Kindersley would like to thank:
Beehive Illustrations (Andy Cooke) for original illustrations; Rose Horridge and Charlotte Oster for picture library services.

Picture credits:
The publisher would like to thank the following for their kind permission to reproduce their photographs:
a=above; c=center; b=below; l=left; r=right; t=top;

Alamy.com: Steve Bloom Images 8-9; 21tl. **Ardea London Ltd:** Ian Beames 27tr; Liz Bomford 12cr; Thomas Dressler 28tl; Jean-Paul Ferrero 20; Ferrero - Labat 3; Chris Knights 43br; Charles McDougal 13; Stefan Meyers 43tl; S. Roberts 19t; Adrian Warren 19cr. **Bruce Coleman Ltd:** Bruce Coleman Inc 17tr, 24; Peter A. Hinchliffe 17tl; Werner Layer 27tl; Orion Press 6-7; Hans Reinhard 26; Pacific Stock 40; Staffan Widstrand 25tr; Gunter Ziesler 25cl. **Corbis:** Tom Brakefield 11; Bryn Cotton / Assignments Photographers 36bl; Michael and Patricia Fogden 25cb; Gallo Images 1, 4cr, 9tr, 28bl; Layne Kennedy 10cr; W. Wayne Lockwood, M. D. 32-33; Steve Kaufman 33br; W. Perry Conway 37br; Paul A. Souders 10tl; Kennan Ward 27br. **Philip Dowell:** 6cb, 7cb. **The Image Bank / Getty Images:** Joseph Van Os 10bl; Art Wolfe 29. ImageState: 18l, 41b; Natural Selection Inc 44. **FLPA - Images of Nature:** Foto Natura Stock 39tl; David Hosking 45tl; Gerard Lacz 22-23, 42; Minden Pictures 22bc, 37tl, 39, 45tr; Mark Newman 37c, 38cl; W. Wisniewski 46. **Nature Picture Library Ltd:** Mark Payne-Gill 14cl, 31tr. **Natural Visions:** Andrew Henley 16tc. **N.H.P.A.:** Ant Photo Library 30tr, 38b; Pete Atkinson 6cra; Mark Bowler 21tr; Martin Harvey 7clb, 22bl, 44tr, 45bl; Daniel Heuclin 25br; Rich Kirchner 7cla; Alberto Nardi 6crb; Rod Planck 48l, r; Jonathan and Angela Scott 8tl; Karl Switak 16bl; David Woodfall 36bkgd. **Oxford Scientific Films:** Clive Bromhall 21cl; Mike & Elvan Habicht 14tr; Mike Hill 4tl; Peter Lillie 21br; Partridge Films Ltd 12tl. **The Photographers' Library:** L & D Jacobs 4-5b. **Powerstock Photolibrary:** 32tr; Brandon Cole 41tr. **Science Photo Library:** Gregory Dimijian 19bl; Phil Dotson 12cl; Adam Jones 5tr; Stephen J. Krasemann 18bkgd; Renee Lynn 28c. Still Pictures: Klein/Hubert 23tl. **Stone / Getty Images:** Daniel J. Cox 34-35, 35br; Paul Harris 35tl; David Myers 14b; Art Wolfe 34tr. **Telegraph Colour Library / Getty Images:** John Downer 30-31; Tony Evans - Timelapse Library Ltd 16-17; Gary Randall 15. **Jerry Young:** 7ca.

Jacket Images: Bruce Coleman Ltd: Bruce Coleman Inc front br. **FLPA - Images of Nature:** David Hosking front b; Minden Pictures front t, back. Still Pictures: Peter Weimann front bl.